MW01089410

I
SAW
HEAVEN

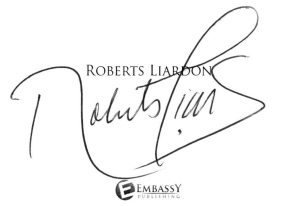

ROBERTS LIARDON

EMBASSY
PUBLISHING

Unless otherwise indicated, all scripture quotations
are taken from the *Holy Bible, New Living Translation,*
copyright © 1996, 2004, 2007 by Tyndale House
Foundation. Used by permission of Tyndale House
Publishers, Inc., Carol Stream, Illinois 60188.
All rights reserved.

Scripture quotations marked NKJV are taken from
the *New King James Version*®. Copyright © 1982 by
Thomas Nelson, Inc. Used by permission.
All rights reserved.

I Saw Heaven
ISBN 978-1-7336062-0-2
Copyright © 1983, 1991, 2010,
2018 by Roberts Liardon
P.O. Box 781888
Orlando, FL 32878
www.robertsliardon.org

Published by Embassy Publishing
P. O. Box 781888
Orlando, FL 32878

Printed in the United States of America. All rights
reserved under International Copyright Law.
Contents and/or cover may not be reproduced in
whole or in part in any form without the express
written consent of the Publisher.

DEDICATION

To my wonderful family: my grand-mother, Gladoylene Moore, my mother Carol Liardon, and my sister and brother-in-law Mike Guthrie and Priscilla Liardon-Guthrie. Their love and faith have and always will give me the inspiration and strength to do my part in bringing Heaven to Earth, as Jesus taught us.

I remember your genuine faith, for you share the faith that first filled your grandmother Lois and your mother, Eunice. And I know that same faith continues strong in you.

2 Timothy 1:5

CONTENTS

FOREWORD
(from my pastor)

Roberts Liardon is a young man who has matured spiritually far beyond his years. As you read this anointed book, remember that God is no respecter of persons.

As a student in Victory Christian School, Roberts provided a consistent model of Christian character. He has been respected by students, teachers, and administrators.

In counseling Roberts early in his ministry, I cautioned him about the danger of pride. Success at such a young age is often spoiled by arrogance. In my estimation, Roberts has been able to handle the rapid progress with God's grace.

You will be blessed, as you read, to know there is a quality life behind these pages. Jesus truly has come to life in this young man.

Rev. Billy Joe Daugherty
Pastor, Victory Christian Center
Tulsa, Oklahoma

Roberts Liardon's life and ministry is having a powerful impact on the body of Christ and appears to be poised to reach a new level in its influence for the Lord's last-day ministry. As I've preached for his growing church, with the students of his Bible school attending, I sense something special is moving upon them. It could be partially by the influence of the vision, which he describes in this book, virtually enmeshing his life from a child.

He is a strong Bible preacher and teacher, also a gatherer of materials of noted men and women of God of the past one hundred years, in an effort to reveal how God does His mighty deeds.

It is my feeling, as Roberts continues to obey God, grow in the Word, build his strong teaching, and perseveres totally committed to the Lord Jesus, his impact will be immeasurable on thousands worldwide.

Sincerely,

Oral Roberts
Newport Beach, California
May 2000

PREFACE

Since Jesus took me to Heaven for a visit when I was eight years old, I have published this story three times. The first edition was printed when I was seventeen, the second edition was printed when I was twenty-five, and the third edition was printed when I was forty-four. To be honest, at fifty-two I am not fully satisfied with any of these versions. My dissatisfaction is not because the story was inaccurately told, but because in each version I tried to explain things and answer questions I thought might be in the mind of the reader.

This new version is unlike all the others because I just tell the story. I have tried to tell it as I experienced it as an eight-year-old and not as I remembered it at seventeen, twenty-five, forty-four, or even at fifty-two years old. I believe that is the best way for you to experience it: through the eyes of a little boy who was captivated by the love and laughter of Jesus.

I will come to visions and revelations of the Lord: I know a man in Christ who fourteen years ago—whether in the body I do not know, or whether out of the body I do not know, God knows—such a one was caught up to the third heaven. And I know such a man—whether in the body or out of the body I do not know, God knows—how he was caught up into Paradise and heard inexpressible words, which it is not lawful for a man to utter.

2 Corinthians 12:1-4 NKJV

1

PULLED UPWARD

I'm eight years old in the summer of 1974, and I'm playing baseball with my friends after school. I realize it's close to dinnertime, so I go home to read my Bible. I want to be able to watch television or go back out and play this evening, but Mom and Grandma have laid down the law: read four chapters in my Bible every day, or no fun. Grandma came to live with us because my grandfather went to Heaven, my father left and divorced Mom when I was five, and all of us, including my mother, are in school. Grandma has us praying too. She says, "If you're going to do anything for God, you're going to have to pray."

I walk into my bedroom, and

before I can reach for my Bible and fall on my bed, something strong comes underneath and around me. It begins to pull me upward. I'm above my house! I look down and see my friend's backyard and my other friends going back to their homes with their baseball bats and gloves.

I'm traveling up through space very, very fast. I must be moving at the speed of light. Even though I'm moving fast, it is quiet and still around me. *It's the Rapture! It's happened!* But I look to my right and left and see no one else. *Well, this couldn't be the Rapture. At least Grandma would be here if it were!* I pass things, but I can't see them clearly. Everything is just blurs.

I wonder where I'm going, and suddenly I land in front of the biggest gate I ever saw in my life. It is very wide and very tall. This gate is one, solid pearl all the way through. It's very shiny. The edges of the gate are carved with a design, but the rest is a glossy, glowing white. I shake myself to see if this is a dream. I walk forward and touch the gate to prove it's real. It is! Then I hear a man say, "This is one of the gates."

I turn to my left and see Jesus. I know it's him, but he doesn't look like any of the pictures I have seen. He is bright and glowing, like no one I've ever seen on Earth. He's so big, about six feet tall. He's not white or black; he's somewhere in between. His light, brown hair comes to his shoulders, and he has a beard — and muscles! He's the perfect man. Everything about him is just right. I know it's not nice to stare, but I can't stop staring at him. My legs crumble, and I fall on my knees in front of him. Everything in me cries for joy. Tears stream down my face. I cannot stop them.

He says, "Now stop the tears. It's time to go through Heaven. I want to give you a tour through Heaven, because I love you so much."

I hear and feel his words at the same time, and his words change me on the inside, like joy exploding. I can't stop crying. He's too wonderful! He says, "No need of tears, but a face full of joy would make me glad." He laughs —a deep belly laugh — and I do too! He reaches down, takes hold of me, and draws me up to stand in front of him. He wipes away my tears with his fingers.

He loves me, and he likes me. I'm not scared at all! I realize who he is, but it isn't like being with a famous person on Earth. I'm totally calm. I look around. It's so beautiful! I don't have any words to describe it.

Jesus takes my hand, and we walk toward the gate. It just lifts up. He didn't ask anyone to open it, and he didn't push a button. The gate just lifts up, and we walk through.

2

GOLD STREETS

I know I'm in Heaven, and the first thing I see is a golden street with golden curbs. The curbs are lined with flowers in all the colors of the rainbow. *If this is Heaven, then this is a golden street I'm standing on!* I look down and make a mad dash for the grass. Jesus turns to say something to me, but I am gone. I am standing on the grass with my eyes and mouth wide open in surprise, looking back at him.

He asks, "What are you doing over there?"

I say, "Golden streets," and look down at them. Some parts look like our gold on Earth, but there are other parts that are as clear as glass. I can see through them.

Jesus laughs. He laughs so hard, I think he never will stop. Finally, he says, "Come here."

I say, "No. These streets are gold. I can't walk on them!"

Jesus motions for me to come to him, saying, "Come on," and he laughs again, even harder. He walks over to get me. "These streets are made for my brothers and sisters to enjoy."

I come to him, and we begin to walk down the golden street. As we walk, I realize that the air in Heaven feels completely different. It's got love, joy, and peace in it, and the wind is amazing. It feels like the Holy Spirit feels back home. Every few moments, a wave flows right through me and everything around me. The flowers hum, and the leaves on the trees move.

It's like the trees are dancing. I have only good thoughts, and everything around me is for me. Nothing is against me. I'm so happy. I feel like I belong here.

I look up and see clouds. I have read about the glory clouds in my Bible and have heard about them in church, but these *are* the glory clouds! I just know everything has a purpose. I don't know the purpose of the glory clouds, but they are something to behold, and I'm sure they have a purpose.

We pass communities with buildings that are offices and places of business. I see people going about their business. They are smiling from ear to ear. Some sing hymns I recognize from Earth, and some sing heavenly songs that I know have a heavenly meaning. People carry little bundles, and some carry books. I notice one woman, because she walks like she's bouncing.

She sees Jesus and stops to talk. She knows I am visiting. She leaves us to go into a store with her bundle of goods, and a few minutes later, out she comes with a book too. I don't see any money, but I know people are doing business.

I think, *People on Earth think that when they get to Heaven, they're going to float around on clouds; but that's not true! That's lazy, and no one here is lazy. We're all going to have jobs to do, but we're going to have fun doing them. Our jobs here are going to be the best we've ever had!*

I see books in Heaven that are also on Earth, and there are songs people sing in Heaven that we sing on Earth. I also see books and hear songs in Heaven that have not come to Earth yet. Somehow, I know it's because no one has paid the price for them.

3

A HEAVENLY MANSION

Jesus and I come to a little town, where I see street signs. All along the way, I see homes of different sizes, styles, and shapes. They fit the person who lives in them. We turn to go up a dirt path, and I try to kick the dirt and make a dust cloud, the way we do in Oklahoma, but the dirt won't budge. It just stays on the ground no matter how hard I kick it. I look up and see a gigantic house that rises above the trees. It looks like a mansion.

Jesus talks to me all the way to the mansion, and when we get to the door, he knocks. (I guess people in Heaven are polite. They don't just float through people's walls and surprise them!) He waits a few minutes and then knocks again. Finally, I hear someone coming to the door. I think, *If Jesus came to my door, I'd answer right away!*

A gentleman cracks the door open and sticks his head out. He sees who it is, opens his door, and says, "How are you doing, Jesus? And how are *you* doing, Roberts?"

What?!!! I almost take off running. *How does he know my name? Only Jesus knows my name!*

I look up at the gentleman and say, "Well, I'm doing okay." And from that point on, as I travel with Jesus, I realize everyone knows my name. They ask, "How are you doing, Roberts?" Because my first name is Roberts with an "s" and not just Robert, I usually have to explain that I am named after Oral Roberts. But everybody in Heaven knows that.

The gentleman says, "Come in," and

we walk inside his house. He looks like he is about thirty years old. I realize that everyone I am seeing in Heaven looks to be about that age. Jesus and I follow him into a living room, and we sit down on a black, velvet couch. Whoa! It reaches around me and cuddles me! I'm so comfortable, I don't have to move once! At home, I always squirm around until I'm comfortable.

The man asks us questions just like people do at home. It's interesting. We talk about how Heaven and Earth move together. The man is aware of his family on Earth, but I'm not sure how much he knows about them. I'm glad he isn't totally cut off from them, though.

After we finish talking, we get up and the man takes Jesus and me through his house, which is huge. It looks like an American house, with curtains on the windows, and it's perfect. It's perfect for this man. It has paintings that are like our modern art and family pictures. There are lots of beautiful plants of all sizes. There are a lot of things I know cost a lot on Earth, and some things I don't recognize. There are different rooms, such as a dining room, a living room, a kitchen, and a den. There is an upstairs, and I am sure there are bedrooms, but we don't go up there. I wonder if people in Heaven lie down and rest.

When we come back to the living room, the man serves me a big fruit to eat. It looks like an apple, but it is red, orange, and yellow mixed together. When I bite into it, it reminds me of a pear, and it's delicious! I never tasted anything like it — not bitter or too sweet — just right. When we say goodbye to the man, he hugs us and kisses us. Then we go out the back door. I don't know why. Probably because it's closer. The back yard is beautiful. There are no fences. I take a deep breath and feel like I'm filled with the wonderful smell of the trees and flowers and grass.

4

ANIMALS AND BOUNCY GRASS

Jesus and I walk over a few small hills, and I see all kinds of animals. *Of course! Earth is like Heaven, so Heaven has animals like ours.* I see a dog, a baby goat, and a lion that looks very strong. There are other kinds of animals in Heaven, but I see them at a distance and don't know what they are. The animals don't run from us or try to attack us. They are calm and peaceful. There is no fear in Heaven!

There are birds singing in the trees, big birds and little birds, and they are all singing the same song. When they stop singing, it seems like they are talking to each other. I can understand what they are singing but not what they are talking about.

The grass is so green! Our green on Earth cannot describe it. It's *very* green — green green. And it's so soft. After I walk on it a bit, I look back and see my footprints disappear. The grass immediately bounces back up! Jesus laughs as I play with it for a while. I jump on it as hard as I can again and again, and it still bounces back! The best part is that I know I will never have to mow it. It's always perfect.

I see a leaf fall from a tree, and it disappears. All the fruit is ripe and perfect for eating. All the leaves are green and the limbs are strong. There isn't one thing wrong in Heaven. And I sense that even I could not get into trouble here. I don't see other kids, but I know they are here.

5

A PRAISE SERVICE

After seeing the animals and playing on the grass, we start walking again. It hits me that Heaven is a real place. Like Earth, it has villages, towns, communities, and homes of all shapes and sizes for people. The light is different, though. It's like God is the source of all the light in the same way a light bulb has this glow all around it. His light is so powerful and full of joy, and it's all around us. The only water I see comes from the River of Life. I guess all the water comes from God's throne. It seems alive.

Everything and everyone in Heaven is perfect, just like Jesus. I love it here! Most of all, I love being with him. He introduces me to more people. We talk about things that happened already and things that will happen in the future. I realize I'm dressed like everyone else. We are in white robes that seem to come from inside us, and people have different colored sashes. Some have their sashes around their waists and some have them over their shoulders. Mine is red and yellow mixed together and is around my waist and my shoulder. Some are wearing jewelry too: necklaces, bracelets, and rings made of gold and gemstones.

We are all healthy and look great. No one is too fat or too skinny. We are all just right. If we had any sickness or handicap or anything wrong with us on Earth, it's gone here in Heaven. I realize that men look like men and women look like women. There are people from countries all over the world, and I can tell the difference between people and angels.

Angels are amazing! I wonder, *How can all those people on Earth think angels are little, half-naked children with wings, floating around?* Angels are huge and really strong! I guess they are about seven to eight feet tall, and some have wings and some don't. They act different around Jesus than we do. They are a lot quieter. People talk with Jesus more. I think, *It's because we get saved and they don't. They've always been holy servants of God. Books and movies at home tell us people become angels when they die or angels can become human. They don't know what they're talking about!*

Jesus and I say goodbye to the people we are talking to and start walking again. I see a big building that looks like one of our convention centers on Earth, but it has this golden glow with sparkles coming out of the top and a little bit is falling all around it. Hundreds of people are going inside. At the door, Jesus and I meet two angels, who start talking to him. I watch their wings, which move a lot. When the wings move, the air makes a musical sound. I guess the feathers are about four feet long. I walk behind one of the angels and try to pull out a feather, but I can't. The angels don't even notice! They just keep talking to Jesus. I guess it's because I'm a little boy.

I walk back over to Jesus, and the angels escort us through the door and down an aisle. As we walk, all kinds of people greet us, shake our hands, and kiss us. Everyone is so happy. The angels lead us to the second row of chairs, where two seats are waiting for us. I look around and feel like I'm in a family reunion, where people haven't seen each other for years. They are hugging and kissing and saying things like, "How are you? Glory to God!" We all love each other so much. It's why we do everything.

I go to our chairs first, and Jesus and I sit down. A holy hush sweeps over the whole building. As we say on Earth, we could hear a pin drop to the ground. I see a stage in front of me, and from the right of it comes hundreds of praisers. They aren't angels, because they are dressed differently, like a formal choir in beautiful robes. Even their hair is perfect. They walk onto the stage smiling, and then suddenly, they begin to praise God. Their hands fly up, their voices are strong and loud, and they all start to dance! *Wow! They aren't like our choirs back home!*

The rest of us can't stop ourselves from jumping up and praising God with them. *This is a hundred times better than our praise services on Earth!* The praisers are wild, praising God, dancing off the stage, and going all over the place. Everyone (including me) jumps up and down and are wild with them. I look at Jesus, and he is standing there, beaming from ear to ear, enjoying every second of it. It is quite a sight. Everything is perfect, even though there are no leaders and we are praising God with everything we've got. The music just gets better and better, greater and greater.

I see my praise to God coming out of my mouth and out of everyone else's mouths, because our praises are glowing, bright, yellow vapors. There are sparkles in it, and I try to catch them, like we do when we blow bubbles on Earth. I watch our praises float up and collect at the top of the building. It seems like we do this for two hours before we stop. As soon as we're quiet, our praises shoot out the top of the building! I think they go to the Throne Room. The praisers make their way back to the stage, line up, straighten their robes, and then file off. The smiles never leave their faces.

Jesus turns to me and says, "How did you like the service?"

"I loved it! But why did you stop it?"

"Because we have other things to do. Now we are heading for the River of Life."

As we leave, I hear people saying that they can't wait for the next praise service, which is starting right away. There is always praise in Heaven.

6

WATER FIGHT

We leave the praise service building, and as we walk on the gold street, I look up and Jesus is crying! "Roberts, I love my people so much, that I would go back to Earth, preach my three years, die, and go to Hell again for just one person —if I had not paid the price for them and if I thought they wanted to come to Heaven. I wouldn't have to know they'd make it. If I just *thought* they'd want to come, I'd do it for them, even if they were the greatest sinner of all."

As we walk, he keeps crying and saying, "I love my people so much. Why don't they take me at my word? Don't they know that I have all power in Heaven and in Earth to back up what

I said? It's so easy. I made it so simple. If my people will just take me at my word, I will do it."

He cries even harder and says, "I don't understand why people say they believe I will do something, but when it doesn't happen when they want it to, they start doubting my word. If they will just believe and say it with confidence, I will do it. I will do it at the right time."

I stop. Tears are streaming down my face too. *I have unbelief! My unbelief hurts Jesus!* I say, "I'm going to do my best to always believe you and never doubt you. I promise." We hug and then walk until we reach a branch of the River of Life. The water is crystal clear. We take off our shoes and walk in. I feel the life go through me. It isn't around me. It's moving through me, and I feel so clean. We are walking *on* the water *in* the water. I sense it has no bottom, but

I'm waist deep in it and am also walking on it. This is wild!

Suddenly, I feel a strong hand on my head, pushing me down, under the water. *Jesus is dunking me!* As soon as he lets go, I come up as fast as I can and splash him with all my might. He is splashing me, and I keep splashing him. *I'm having a water fight with Jesus!* We are both laughing so hard. He's my very best friend forever!

7

CLOUD OF WITNESSES

Jesus and I finish playing in the River of Life and get out. It feels like a big hair dryer is blowing on us, drying our clothes. We put on our shoes and start walking again. We walk by a wall of a city and I see something that is funny. It looks like football stands along the wall, but the stands are facing out from the city, toward Earth.

Lots of people are in the stands. They are wearing all kinds of hats — some are like baseball caps — and they are waving little flags. All of them are yelling things like, "Go! Do this! Do that! Go get 'em! That's right! You can do it!"

Half-time comes, and everyone hits their knees in prayer. Half-time is prayer time. As soon as it's over, they get back up and start cheering again. *I see. My real family is in Heaven and Earth. This must be the cloud of witnesses the Bible talks about. It will be nice to know they are here, cheering me on, when I go back home.*

8

THRONE ROOM

Next I see a massive space that has borders. Lightning bolts are being thrown from the back of it, and rumblings and thunder are coming from inside. I always ask Jesus when I have a question, but this time I think, *I wonder what this is?* And his answer comes into my mind immediately: "It's the Throne Room of God." *Wow!*

We continue walking toward it, and I count seven rows of flowers in front. They line the pathway up to where you go in. The colors of the flowers are changing constantly, in all the colors of the rainbow, and I notice that every flower, bud, and leaf all look the same size. I count twelve trees. They are not like our trees on Earth. Each has a different fruit. None of the fruits look like anything I have seen on Earth. The trees are in a design.

As we walk closer to the front, I see two angels standing there. Each holds a big, strong sword, and the blades have flames of fire. Their swords touch, and sparks fly from them. Wow!

9

STOREHOUSES

Jesus and I turn from the Throne Room area, and I see three large buildings, like storage facilities, about five to six hundred yards away. The buildings are very long and wide. They remind me of chicken houses back home, only a little bigger. When we walk into the first one, I am shocked at what I see. There are body parts everywhere. Some are hanging on the walls, some are in packages on shelves. I'm surprised it doesn't feel weird. I think, *This building has all the parts of the human body that people on Earth need. No one in Heaven needs them.*

Jesus says, "These are the unclaimed

blessings. This building should not be full. It should be emptied every single day. You should come in here with faith and get the needed parts for you and the people you'll come in contact with that day." As we walk around, I see arms, hands, legs, feet, skin, eardrums — and blue, green, and brown eyeballs. I'm thinking, *If we just ask in faith, God will fix us!*

Toward the back of this building, Jesus sees someone and starts talking to them. I'm continuing to explore and find something like a medicine cabinet up on a wall. I open it and see pill bottles. I reach up, get one, and look at the label. It says, "Peace." I put it back and take down another one. The label says, "Great Joy." As I put that one back on the shelf, I notice that another says, "Love." Then I grab one and stare at the label. It says, "Overdose of the Holy

44

Ghost." *My land, overdoses kill people!* But then I think, *Well, the Holy Ghost won't kill you. He'll just translate you!* Now I'm laughing at my own joke.

I hear Jesus laugh. He sees me holding the Holy Ghost Overdose pill bottle. I put the bottle back and close the cabinet door. We are still laughing, and Jesus is leaning back, roaring with laughter now. At times, I think he will collapse, he laughs so loud and strong. I think, *There is no sickness here. We are crazy to think anything bad comes from God.*

Jesus motions me to come, and we walk through a door and into the next building. I see angels working. They are very busy, moving all around. They pull files out of big file cabinets, check things off, bring things to other angels, and are all over the place. They don't even notice Jesus and me. I guess this is the Filing Room.

Jesus walks over to a file cabinet, pulls open a drawer, and pulls out a file. He hands it to me, and I read the label: Kenneth Roberts Liardon. I open it and see a list, and it goes on for several pages. I look at it fast and close it up so we can go on.

10

I Am Ordained

We leave the storehouses and walk for a while, but we aren't talking. I am thinking about all the amazing things I have seen.

Jesus stops, turns to me, and puts both my hands in one of his. He puts his other hand on top of my head. "Roberts, I am calling you to a great work. I am ordaining you to a great work. You will have to run like no one else, preach like no one else, be different from everyone else. Hard times will come, but take them as stepping stones not as stumbling blocks. Go with power and with faith. I will be beside you everywhere you go. Go, go, go like no one else has gone. Go and do as I have done." At the first "Go," I feel warm and tingly, and every time he says, "go" it gets warmer, until I feel really hot.

Jesus removes his hand from my head and releases my hands as he steps back from me. My hands are very red. Then Jesus shows me a screen, and on it I see parts of my life from the day I was born until now. Then it shows me different times of my life until I come back to Heaven.

On the screen, I see people who will come into my life and affect it greatly and those I will affect greatly. He tells me their first names and last initials only. I see myself preaching in different places and my ministry in the future. I know there are many things I cannot tell anyone. It's all up to God and his timing. I'm supposed to trust him and obey him. I am really excited by all the people I am leading to Jesus as I watch.

I don't want to miss any of them, even if it means I'll live to be an old man.

The screen goes away, and Jesus says, "I want you to return to Earth and not be like anyone you have met or known, and do exactly what I have called you to do. I've placed inside you the ability and the strength to do it." He hugs me and kisses me. It's time for me to go back home. I don't want to stay, because I have so much to do on Earth. I have to lead many souls to Jesus!

I leave him and walk toward the nearest gate. Jesus says, "Roberts!" I turn and see him, tears streaming down his face and arms outstretched. "I love you."

Instantly, I am moving through space like I did before, but this time my angel is with me. He introduces himself and says, "I am the one who is with you. I am the one who stands with you. I am the one who assists you. I am the one who protects you. I will be with you, even throughout eternity, and I will stand by your side. And, there will be other angels who will come and go throughout your life."

I am back in my bedroom.

I think about all I have seen and experienced in Heaven. I have no doubt that it really happened. For several hours, I still feel the heat and fire all through me and on me. I know I must wait for the right moment before I tell anyone, so I pick up my Bible and begin reading my four chapters. I want to be able to play after dinner.

11

GENERALS

Now I am twelve, watching the television show, *Laverne and Shirley*, by myself in our living room. I notice a bright light coming through our front door and assume it is the sun, but something about it is different. I stare at it because it seems too bright to be the sun. Suddenly, a foot and a leg come through the light, and then Jesus comes through. He takes two steps toward me, and the whole room seems to move about two hundred yards away. I am still hearing the television show, but my focus is on Jesus.

He says, "Hello, Roberts!"

"Hi, Jesus!" I am so happy to see him! *Why is he here?*

He walks over and sits down beside me on the couch. "I want you to study the lives of my generals in my great army throughout time. Know them like the back of your hand. Know why some succeeded and some failed, for there will come a generation who will need to know what I show you, if you will be faithful to do what I've asked you to do this day. For in those days, you will help save, salvage, and unwrap gifts for those whom you will meet, who will have diverse responsibilities throughout the Earth. If you will do what I've asked you today, you will meet the generals of your lifetime and they will become your friends. If you are faithful in this, I will promote you. There will be a day that people will consider you to be a father to them. Receive them, instruct them, show them love, and then let them see the demonstration of my Spirit."

Jesus gets up and walks back out our front door. I turn to continue watching *Laverne and Shirley*. I don't want to think about what he said, because I don't like to study, and he wants me to study fat, old, bald preachers. Some alive and some dead. That sounds really boring!

Eventually, I know I have to do what Jesus told me to do or I will get in big trouble. I find the biography of one of the "fat, old, bald preachers" called Smith Wigglesworth, which my grandma gave me. I force myself to sit down and read, and I am shocked. I really like it! I don't want to stop reading it and can't get enough of this stuff. I read everything I can find in our family library, my school library, and the public library on these people Jesus calls "generals."

After a while, I see what the problem is. The stories I hear about these generals who have died, what preachers are saying about them, are not the same as what I am reading. In fact, sometimes I hear a preacher combine stories from a couple of generals' lives and make it about another general — and that didn't happen to that general at all! I know I must be extremely careful to find out exactly what happened in these generals' lives, so I can set the record straight.

As I'm reading about these generals, the Holy Spirit helps me and teaches me so I can get it right. He asks me questions. "Did you notice this? Do you understand how they said that? See how they moved with me that way?" He shows me scenes in my mind and says, "This is the way it was. I was there." *The Holy Spirit is my history teacher.*

I have to give up some things I really like to do. I can't spend as much time with my friends, and I have to give up sports and watching television. Sometimes it's hard, but most of the time it's great. These generals really know how to deal with the devil. They aren't afraid of him or demons at all. Too many Christians I know just seem to run from him, but these guys run after him and stop him!

These generals really win souls and get so many people healed and delivered from demons. They lead people to Jesus and then get them baptized in the Holy Spirit. There are miracles happening all the time, wherever they go. Awesome healing miracles! And some of the mistakes they make are things we need to know today, so we can avoid the bad stuff. Most of all, I see what they did right, like Jesus said, "why they succeeded." We need to know those things too. Then we can succeed in whatever he tells us to do.

I read all about John Alexander Dowie, Charles G. Finney, David Livingston, William Booth, Maria Woodworth-Etter, John G. Lake, Aimee Semple McPherson, and many others. Kathryn Kuhlman is still alive but old. I always have a book on them with me, at home and at school. I find old newspaper articles on them in the library. Then I realize something: Some people who worked with them in their ministries are still alive. Some of the generals had children or grandchildren, and they are still alive. I need to call them and interview them!

People who know these generals or are related to them talk to me because I'm a kid. Some of them are glad to have a teenager around or on the phone who is interested in them and the general I ask them about. I record as many conversations as I can with my tape recorder and always have a notebook to take notes.

Mom and Grandma are concerned. I can tell. They wonder why I'm not out playing with my friends like I used to, but I don't want to tell them what Jesus did and said yet. They don't even know about my visit to Heaven. I just tell them I really like reading.

I come home from school, and Grandma and Mom are waiting for me. Grandma says that today she answered the telephone, and it was a long-distance call from another country. The person wanted to talk to me. They thought I was much older than I am.

I tell them what Jesus told me to do. They want me to talk to our pastor, so I do. I don't tell him about my experiences with Jesus. I just tell him what I feel called to do. He is excited about it.

12

MY STORY IS FOR YOU

I was eight years old when I went to Heaven, and it was not my idea. Later, Jesus walked into my living room, and I wasn't even thinking about him. Every powerful, supernatural occurrence in my life has been God's idea not mine. There is great safety in that!

A long time ago, I chose to let God decide what supernatural experiences I have. When I have one, I go immediately to the Bible to validate it or reject it. If I'm not sure about it, I put it on the shelf and wait until I know for certain what the Holy Spirit and the Word say about it.

Personally, I would love for you

to experience Heaven like I did as a little boy. I wouldn't deny anyone that adventure with Jesus! But it's not up to me. It's up to Him. If you are a believer and Jesus is Lord of your life, then I hope you enjoyed reading about my trip to Heaven, that it gave you a richer, deeper picture of our wonderful, amazing Savior.

If you are not a believer, and my story gave you a desire to go to Heaven when your life on Earth is finished, let's make sure *you* get there!

How do I get to Heaven?

I am so glad you asked!

Jesus is the only way you get to Heaven. He connects you to God, and that is awesome. God our Father is awesome! Sometimes you hear His voice, but at all times His peace on the inside of you lets you know that He is with you. You can have this intimate relationship with Him only through Jesus, because He's the one who died for your sins. Jesus made a great and painful sacrifice to show how much God loves you — no matter what you've done — and He wants you to be His child.

To be with Him forever and go to Heaven, all you have to do is pray this prayer (from Romans 10:9-10) and mean it with all your heart:

"Father, thank You for sending Jesus to die for my sins, and I receive Your forgiveness through His great sacrifice. I believe You raised Jesus from the dead to give me a new life with You, and so I declare that Jesus is my Lord forever. Thank You for saving me! Amen."

To understand what it means to be
a child of God and where you go from
here, find a good Christian church,
where they will teach you the Bible,
pray for you, and encourage you in
your new life with God.

Welcome to the family of God, and
may He richly bless you in every area
of your life!

Roberts Liardon

I became God's child on

_____

Date

_____

Name

Scriptures About Heaven

Pulled Upward — Or Just a Look

Enoch lived 365 years, walking in close fellowship with God. Then one day he disappeared, because God took him.

Genesis 5:23-24

Jacob found a stone to rest his head against and lay down to sleep. As he slept, he dreamed of a stairway that reached from the earth up to heaven. And he saw the angels of God going up and down the stairway.

Genesis 28:11-12

On July 31 of my thirtieth year, while I was with the Judean exiles beside the Kebar River in Babylon, the heavens were opened and I saw visions of God.

Ezekiel 1:1

Then he said [Jesus to the twelve], "I tell you the truth, you will all see heaven open and the angels of God going up and down on the Son of Man, the one who is the stairway between heaven and earth."

John 1:51

After saying this, he was taken up into a cloud while they were watching, and they could no longer see him. As they strained to see him rising into heaven, two white-robed men suddenly stood among them. "Men of Galilee," they said, "why are you standing here staring into heaven? Jesus has been taken from you into heaven, but someday he will return from heaven in the same way you saw him go!"

Acts 1:9-11

I was caught up to the third heaven fourteen years ago...and heard things so astounding that they cannot be expressed in words, things no human is allowed to tell.

2 Corinthians 12:2-4

Pearl Gates, Gold Streets, Treasures, and Joy

The wall of the city was built on foundation stones inlaid with twelve precious stones.

The twelve gates were made of pearls—each gate from a single pearl! And the main street was pure gold, as clear as glass.

Revelation 21:19, 21

Store your treasures in heaven, where moths and rust cannot destroy, and thieves do not break in and steal.

Matthew 6:20

Jesus told him, "If you want to be perfect, go and sell all your possessions and give the money to the poor, and you will have treasure in heaven. Then come, follow me."

Matthew 19:21

In Your presence is fullness of joy;
At Your right hand are pleasures forevermore.

Psalm 16:11 NKJV

"He will wipe every tear from their eyes, and there will be no more death or sorrow or crying or pain. All these things are gone forever."

Revelation 21:4

Houses, Animals, Birds, and Food

In My Father's house are many mansions; if it were not so, I would have told you. I go to prepare a place for you. And if I go and prepare a place for you, I will come again and receive you to Myself; that where I am, there you may be also.

John 14:2-3 NKJV

Then I saw heaven opened, and a white horse was standing there.

Revelation 19:11

In the center and around the throne were four living beings, each covered with eyes, front and back. The first of these living beings was like a lion; the second was like an ox; the third had a human face; and the fourth was like an eagle in flight.

Revelation 4:6-7

Then I saw an angel standing in the sun; and he cried with a loud voice, saying to all the birds that fly in the midst of heaven, "Come and gather together for the supper of the great God."

Revelation 19:17 NKJV

On each side of the river grew a tree of life, bearing twelve crops of fruit, with a fresh crop each month. The leaves were used for medicine to heal the nations.

Revelation 22:1-2

And the angel said to me, "Write this: Blessed are those who are invited to the wedding feast of the Lamb."

Revelation 19:9

Trees, Clothes, and the River of Life

After this I saw a vast crowd, too great

to count, from every nation and tribe and people and language, standing in front of the throne and before the Lamb. They were clothed in white robes and held palm branches in their hands.

Revelation 7:9

The seven angels who were holding the seven plagues came out of the Temple. They were clothed in spotless white linen with gold sashes across their chests.

Revelation 15:6

She has been given the finest of pure white linen to wear. For the fine linen represents the good deeds of God's holy people.

Revelation 19:8

The armies of heaven, dressed in the finest of pure white linen, followed him on white horses.

Revelation 19:14

Then the angel showed me a river with the water of life, clear as crystal, flowing from the throne of God and of the Lamb. It flowed down the center of the main street. On each side of the river grew a tree of life, bearing twelve crops of fruit, with a fresh crop each month. The leaves were used for medicine to heal the nations.

Revelation 22:1-2

Books

You have collected all my tears in your bottle.

You have recorded each one in your book.

Psalm 56:8

You saw me before I was born.

Every day of my life was recorded in your book.

Psalm 139:16

"Nevertheless do not rejoice in this, that the spirits are subject to you, but rather rejoice because your names are written in heaven."

Luke 10:20 NKJV

All who are victorious will be clothed in white. I will never erase their names from the Book of Life, but I will announce before my Father and his angels that they are mine.

Revelation 3:5

I saw still another mighty angel coming down from heaven, clothed with a cloud. And a rainbow was on his head, his face was like the sun, and his feet like pillars of fire. He had a little book open in his hand.

Revelation 10:1-2 NKJV

And all the people who belong to this world worshiped the beast. They are the ones whose names were not written in the Book of Life that belongs to the Lamb who was slaughtered before the world was made.

Revelation 13:8

I saw the dead, both great and small, standing before God's throne. And the books were opened, including the Book of Life. And the dead were judged according

to what they had done, as recorded in the
books.

Family in Heaven

Therefore [because of the heroes of faith mentioned in chapter 11], *since we are surrounded by such a huge crowd of witnesses to the life of faith, let us strip off every weight that slows us down, especially the sin that so easily trips us up.*

You have come to Mount Zion, to the city of the living God, the heavenly Jerusalem, and to countless thousands of angels in a joyful gathering. You have come to the assembly of God's firstborn children, whose names are written in heaven. You have come to God himself, who is the judge over all things. You have come to the spirits of the righteous ones in heaven who have now been made perfect.

For this reason I bow my knees to the Father of our Lord Jesus Christ, from whom the whole family in heaven and earth is named.

Ephesians 3:14-15 NKJV

In the same way, there is more joy in heaven over one lost sinner who repents and returns to God than over ninety-nine others who are righteous and haven't strayed away!

Luke 15:7

Note about Storehouses

Chapter 9 was the only one I could not find verses of Scripture to completely verify my experience. Hebrews 1:14 says angels serve us, the heirs of salvation, and Luke 10:20 says our names are written in Heaven. However, I could find nothing to confirm that Heaven contains a storehouse filled with body parts, along with pills for mental and emotional problems.

Perhaps Jesus was showing me something that would cement into my eight-year-old brain the truth that He desires to heal all manner of sickness, disease, oppression, depression, and organ defects or missing organs; that when we pray in faith and receive with thanksgiving, we will be healed. That certainly is His message to us then and now, and the Gospels confirm that He healed every ailment and cast out every demon presented to Him during three years of earthly ministry.

I chose to keep this chapter in the book because it supports the truth that "by His stripes we were healed" (1 Peter 2:24), and it encourages our faith in a loving God, whose desire is always to make us whole.

Angels, the Lord's Throne, and Worship

Therefore, angels are only servants— spirits sent to care for people who will inherit salvation.

Hebrews 1:14

As they flew, their wings sounded to me like waves crashing against the shore or like the voice of the Almighty or like the shouting of a mighty army. When they stopped, they let down their wings. As they stood with wings lowered, a voice spoke from beyond the crystal surface above them.

Above this surface was something that looked like a throne made of blue lapis lazuli. And on this throne high above was a figure whose appearance resembled a man. From what appeared to be his waist up, he looked like gleaming amber, flickering like a fire. And from his waist down, he looked like a burning flame, shining with splendor. All around him was a glowing halo, like a rainbow shining in the clouds on a rainy day. This is what the glory of the Lord looked like to me. When I saw it, I fell face down on the ground, and I heard someone's voice speaking to me.

Ezekiel 1:24-28

I saw a throne in heaven and someone sitting on it. The one sitting on the throne was as brilliant as gemstones—like jasper and carnelian. And the glow of an emerald circled his throne like a rainbow. Twenty-four thrones surrounded him, and twenty-four elders sat on them. They were all clothed in white and had gold crowns on their heads. From the throne came flashes of lightning and the rumble of thunder. And in front of the throne were seven torches with burning flames. This is the sevenfold Spirit of God. In front of the throne was a shiny sea of glass, sparkling like crystal.

The twenty-four elders fall down and worship the one sitting on the throne (the

one who lives forever and ever). And they
lay their crowns before the throne.

Revelation 4:2-6, 10

And when he took the scroll, the four
living beings and the twenty-four elders
fell down before the Lamb. Each one had
a harp, and they held gold bowls filled with
incense, which are the prayers of God's
people.

Revelation 5:8

Then I looked again, and I heard the
voices of thousands and millions of angels
around the throne and of the living beings
and the elders. And they sang in a mighty
chorus:

"Worthy is the Lamb who was
slaughtered—

> *to receive power and riches*
> *and wisdom and strength*
> *and honor and glory and blessing."*

Revelation 5:11-12

About the Author

Dr. Roberts Liardon is an author, public speaker, spiritual leader, church historian, and humanitarian. He was called into the ministry at a very young age, preaching his first public sermon at the age of thirteen and lecturing on *God's Generals* in Christian colleges and universities at age fifteen.

From age sixteen, he has utilized every platform to preach the Gospel of Jesus Christ, bring maturity to the Church, and encourage those in ministry. He has produced radio, television, and Internet programs, and has also authored over eighty books, which have been translated into over sixty languages and to date have sold 16.5 million copies.

Dr. Liardon has established many churches and accredited Bible schools and is now building Embassy International Church in Orlando, Florida, an apostolic center to serve his community and the nations. It is also the headquarters of the Embassy Global Network, which provides a gathering place of support and encouragement for ministries and leaders.

In great demand as a speaker and mentor to pastors and leaders worldwide, Dr. Liardon has ministered in over 127 nations and loves to pray, teach the Word of God, and prophesy to bless God's people. He speaks to a current generation of believers who want to draw closer to the heart and mind of God and impact their communities and the nations through the Gospel of Jesus Christ.

You may contact Dr. Liardon at:

Roberts Liardon Ministries
www.robertsliardon.com
Facebook: Roberts Liardon Official
Twitter: Roberts Liardon
Instagram: robertsliardon_official

U.S. Office:
Roberts Liardon Ministries
P.O. Box 781888

Orlando, FL 32878
Email: Admin@robertsliardon.org

UK and Europe Office:
Roberts Liardon Ministries
UK, 22 Notting Hill Gate, Suite 125
London W11 3JE, UK
Email: Admin@robertsliardon.org

Three best-selling books in one,
updated for you today!

Run to the Battle:
Jesus was anointed for action, and so is His body. It's time for Christians to be fervent in prayer and strong in the Spirit, to run to the fight and win.

The Invading Force:
For the Church to reach the uttermost parts of the Earth, Spirit-led believers need to know how to wage war on the offensive.

A Call to Action:
Great spiritual warriors build their lives on the Word of God and do mighty exploits. They know how to hear God's instructions and carry them out in His power.

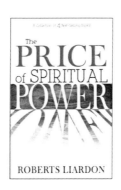

Four favorites in one volume!

Holding to the Word of the Lord:
How to persevere and keep your faith in the
prophetic word God has spoken to you.

The Quest for Spiritual Hunger:
Experience a more intimate
relationship with God.

The Price of Spiritual Power:
Lights your path to holiness
and greater authority.

Spiritual Timing:
How to do the right thing at the right time.

Final APPROACH

THE ADVENTURE OF END-TIMES LIVING

ROBERTS LIARDON

"The End Times are not just about strange signs and unbearable news but the opportunities and adventures of reaping the final End Times harvest."

—Roberts Liardon

These days should be:

- **No hiding – bold living**
- **No hoarding – abundant living**
- **No survival – victorious living**

You will learn how to be a nightmare to the devil while fulfilling your role in these exiting days.

Dr. R.T. Kendall writes: *"You will have a hard time putting this book down. This very interesting and most readable book will bless you, encourage you and make you glad you are living in such a time as this!"*

Roberts Liardon's grandmother, Gladoylene Moore, and her husband LeBasker pioneered churches in North Carolina and received God's vision for a ministry in California

This inspirational story will encourage you to follow God's plan for your life. Discover:

- How God speaks through dreams and visions.
- Effective ministry as a married couple.
- How to pray powerfully in God's Spirit.
- Ways to pray for the sick and cast out devils.
- What to do when you miss an opportunity.
- Ways to break the curse of poverty on your life.

Take a spiritual journey with "Gram" that will deepen your walk with the Lord and birth a new dimension of effective prayer in you.

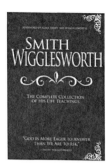

Another one-of-a-kind minister!

God confirmed Smith Wigglesworth's ministry through powerful signs, wonders, and miracles:

- **Restoration of hearing and sight**
- **Creative formation of missing limbs**
- **Disappearance of benign and cancerous growths**
- **Violently insane restored to mental health**
- **Raising several people from the dead**

As you read, you will also see that Wigglesworth's messages and revelation from the Word of God continue to provide spiritual, emotional, mental, physical, relational, and financial healing today.

Be inspired and build a fortress of faith in God as you read about the life and ministry of this awesome man of God!

*The extraordinary life of John G. Lake,
one of the most powerful healing
evangelists of the last century.*

His ministry spanned two continents and included countless conversions, healings, and deliverances. He established hundreds of churches and ministries.

His Spokane Healing Rooms are unique in the archives of medicine and miracles. Lake documented 100,000 healing miracles in five years, and Spokane was declared the healthiest city in the US. Along with medical doctors, nurses, and hospitals, the mayor credited John G. Lake.

Here are his own stirring words! His dynamic messages are at your fingertips in this inspiring 992-page volume.

Kathryn Kuhlman was one of a kind!

Perhaps the most fascinating women of the last century, her miraculous healing ministry spanned half of it.

Read about the countless thousands who were healed in her presence, often without her laying a hand on them.

Learn of her vitality and joy, her tragedies and triumphs, and how she used them all to draw closer to Jesus.

She allowed the Holy Spirit to become her best Friend and greatest Teacher — and you can too!

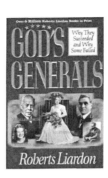

Twelve compelling biographies of some of the most powerful ministers to ever ignite the fires of revival: *John Alexander Dowie, Maria Woodworth-Etter, Evan Roberts, Charles Parham, William J. Seymour, John G. Lake, Aimee Semple-McPherson, Smith Wigglesworth, William Branham, Jack Coe, A.A. Allen,* and *Kathryn Kuhlman.*

Roberts Liardon faithfully chronicles their lives, including their revelations from the Bible, their discoveries about moving in the power of the Holy Spirit, and many revealing photos. He also draws crucial life applications for *you* from the lives of these mighty warriors.

God's Generals will help you learn to obey the Spirit's leading, which will keep your ministry powerful and your life successful!

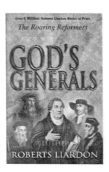

Every generation needs a Reformation!

In this second volume of the *God's Generals* series, Roberts Liardon introduces you to six men, who fought to restore the beliefs and practices of the early church: John Wycliffe, John Hus, Martin Luther, John Calvin; John Knox, and George Fox.

These men pioneered dramatic changes in the thinking and understanding of Christians, giving their lives for the freedom of worship and the Bibles we read in our own languages today.

Journey with them through periods of revelation and persecution. As you read their stories and view their precious and revealing portraits, you'll discover people who gave it all for God.

Dr. Oral Roberts wrote: "A monumental work to stir men's souls."

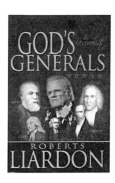

In this third volume of the *God's Generals* series, Roberts Liardon follows the faith journeys and personal lives of some of the most powerful preachers ever to ignite the fires of revival:

John and Charles Wesley, George Whitefield, Jonathan Edwards, Francis Ashbury, Peter Cartwright, Charles Finney, Dwight L. Moody, William and Catherine Booth, and Billy Graham.

Learn how to fulfill God's call while experiencing the joy of being led by the Holy Spirit to lead others to Jesus Christ.

These revivalists will inspire you and revitalize your ministry!

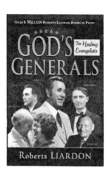

In this fourth volume of the *God's Generals* series, Roberts Liardon chronicles the great healing evangelists of the Twentieth Century.

Glean from the lives of such paragons of faith as Oral Roberts, Lester Sumrall, Charles and Frances Hunter, George Jeffreys, and F. F. Bosworth.

These revivalists will inspire you to step out in faith, have courage in spiritual battle, experience the joy of winning souls to the Lord, pursue Him for healing and miracles, and fulfill all He has called you to accomplish.

As you read about the lives of these ministry pioneers, your faith for signs and wonders will grow. See how God's mighty hand can move in your ministry today!

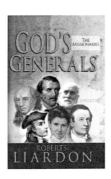

In this fifth volume of the *God's Generals* series, Roberts Liardon reveals the joys and heartaches in the lives of some of the great missionaries — many you may never have heard about. They risked their lives to take the Gospel to foreign and sometimes dangerous tribes and nations.

You will be powerfully motivated as you read of Nikolaus Ludwig von Zinzendorf, David Brainerd, David Livingstone, Adoniram Judson, Hudson Taylor, Hiram Bingham, Amy Carmichael, and Jonathan Goforth.

The sacrifice and courage of these spiritual pioneers are sure to stoke the fires of your faith and revive within your heart a spirit of missions and compassion for the lost.

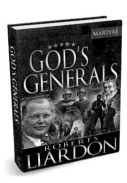

In this sixth volume of the *God's Generals* series, Roberts Liardon is honored to present those who paid the ultimate price. They loved Jesus Christ, His people, and unbelievers more than their own lives.

Some of them will be familiar; others will be unknown to you. But the precious sacrifice of each will pierce your heart and change you forever.

The book includes profiles on biblical and ancient martyrs, martyrs through the centuries, and those who gave their lives in the Philippines, Iraq, Libya, and Syria in recent years.

Their inspirational testimonies, acts of courage, and even seasons of doubt will encourage you and bring a new awareness of the persecuted church, past and present.

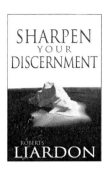

SHARPEN
YOUR
DISCERNMENT

ROBERTS
LIARDON

Sharpen your discernment, and you won't marry the wrong person or get taken by a Christian crook!

We all know people we would call wise, prudent, or discerning. What sets these individuals apart? They walk in the guidance of God. You can too!

From the Scriptures, Roberts Liardon sets you on the path to pursuing a life marked by wisdom. With this knowledge and insight, you can:

- **Go deeper in being led by the Spirit of God.**
- **Develop a habit of successful decision making.**
- **Defeat spiritual forces of evil in your life.**
- **Discover the immense power in daily prayer and Bible-reading.**